ChordBuddy Guitar Method: Volume I

Index

Introduction Unit: Getting to Know the Guitar	Page 2
Vocabulary	Page 4
Unit 1: Quarter Strum Pattern	Page 6
Unit 2: Quarter Strum in 3/4 Time	Page 8
Unit 3: Down/Up Strum Pattern	Page 10
Unit 4: Pick Strum Pattern	Page 12
Unit 5: Alternate Pick Strum Pattern	Page 14
Unit 6: Pop Strum Pattern	Page 16
Unit 7: Progress Check	Page 18

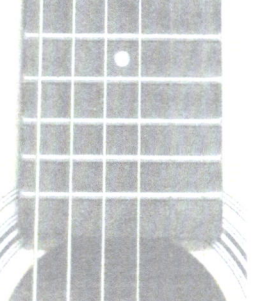

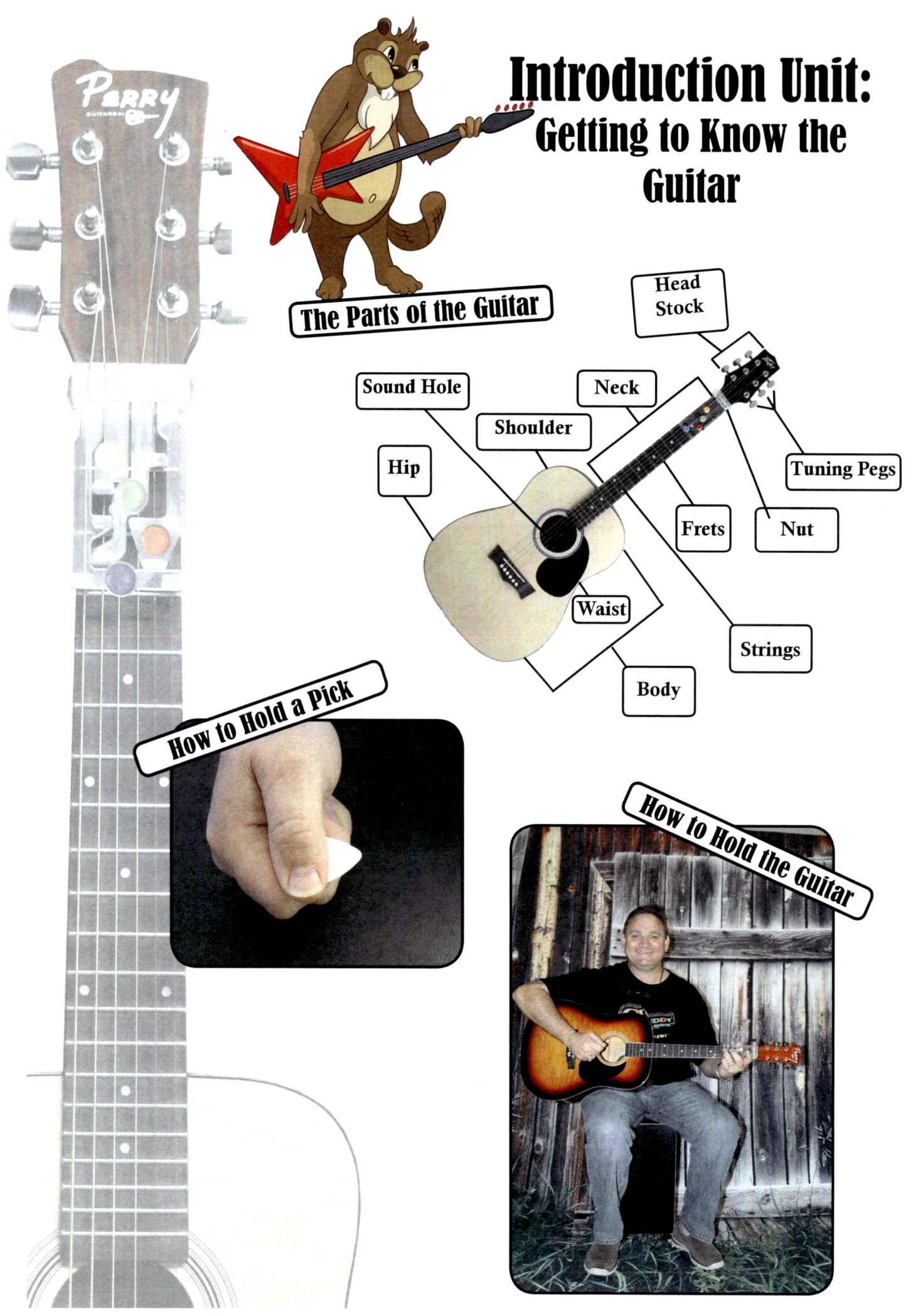

Getting to Know the Guitar

Name of the Strings

Order of the strings
- E- 6th string
- A- 5th string
- D- 4th string
- G- 3rd string
- B- 2nd string
- E- 1st string

Putting on the ChordBuddy
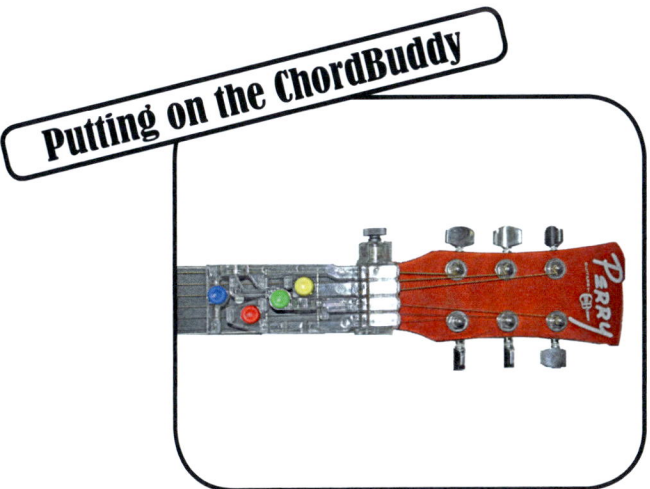

Proper ChordBuddy Angle

The ChordBuddy Chords
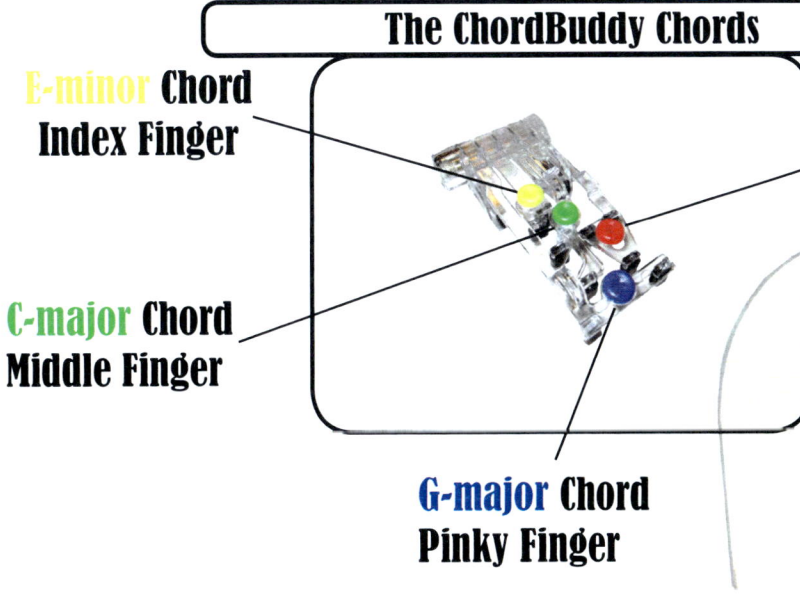

- **E-minor** Chord — Index Finger
- **C-major** Chord — Middle Finger
- **D-major** Chord — Ring Finger
- **G-major** Chord — Pinky Finger

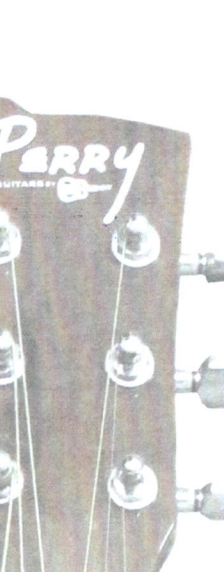

Vocabulary

Chord
In music a chord is a set of three or more notes that are played at the same time. The ChordBuddy allows you to easily play the G Major, C Major, D Major, and E minor chords. A chord has a root/bass note, followed by the 3rd and 5th note of the chord.

Tuning
Each guitar string is assigned its own note. Tuning a guitar is when you check that the open string (string ringing freely) is playing the correct sound. If a string is high it is sharp, if a string is low then it is flat.

Strumming
This is a way of playing a string instrument. A strum is a sweeping action where the pick brushes past several strings in order to set them all into motion.

Picking or Plucking a String
This is a way of playing a string instrument. Picking sets an individual string into motion to produce an audible note.

Vocabulary

Time Signature
This is located at the beginning of a song as a time symbol or stacked numerals, such as 4/4 or 3/4. A time signature specifies how many beats are in each measure and which note value receives one beat. For example: 3/4 - The top number three tells us that there are three beats in each measure, and the bottom 4 tells us that the quarter note receives the beat.

Metronome
A device that makes regular beats or clicks. Metronomes are set in beats per minute (bpm). Example: 80bpm

Tempo
The speed or pace of a song. Tempo is important in music because it can affect the mood and difficulty of a song. It is found at the start of a song and is listed as a number next to a note followed by beats per measure (bpm).
Example: ♩ = 140 The metronome tempo is 140bpm. There are 140 beats in every minute.

Repeat Sign- :||
This is a way of playing a string instrument. A strum is a sweeping action where the pick brushes past several strings in order to set them all into motion.

Unit 1: Quarter Strum

Tuning the Guitar: If a string is low and flat, it needs to be made higher to be in tune. If a string is high and sharp, it needs to be made lower to be in tune.

Order of the Strings:
E- 6th string
A- 5th string
D- 4th string
G- 3rd string
B- 2nd string
E- 1st string

Warm-up 1A

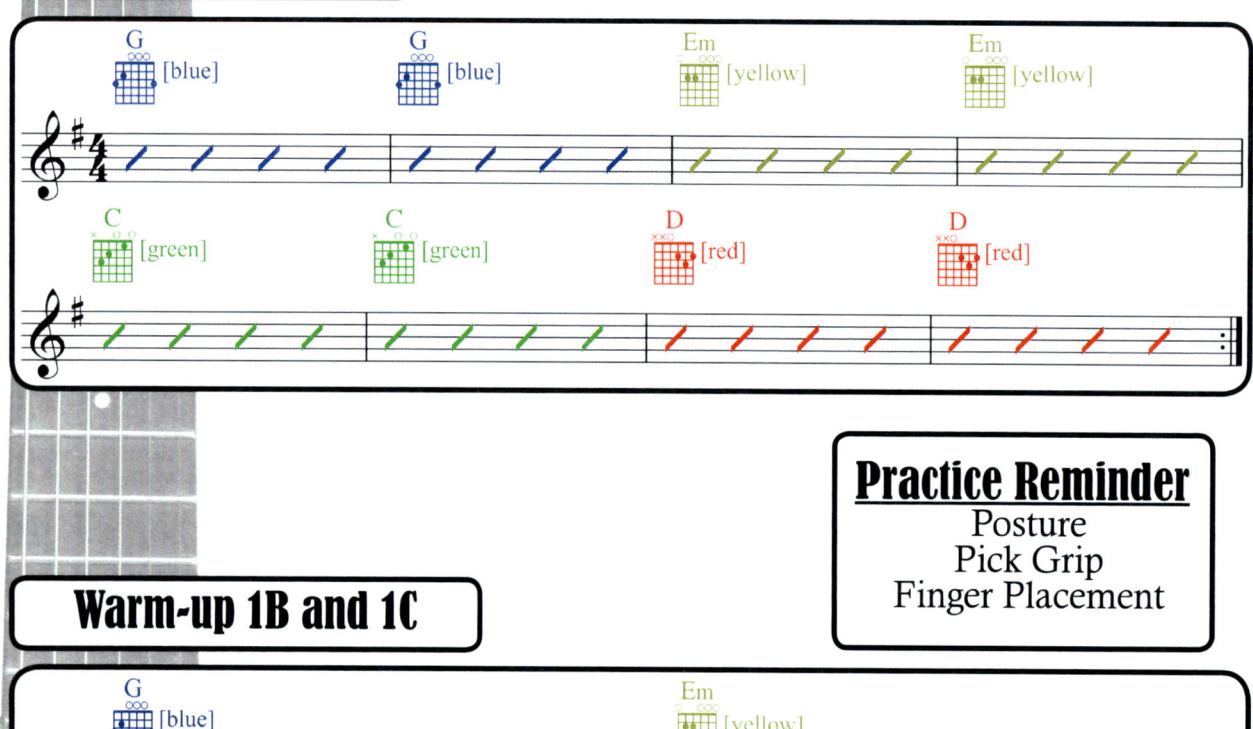

Practice Reminder
Posture
Pick Grip
Finger Placement

Warm-up 1B and 1C

6

Quarter Strum

Tom Dooley 2-Chord Song

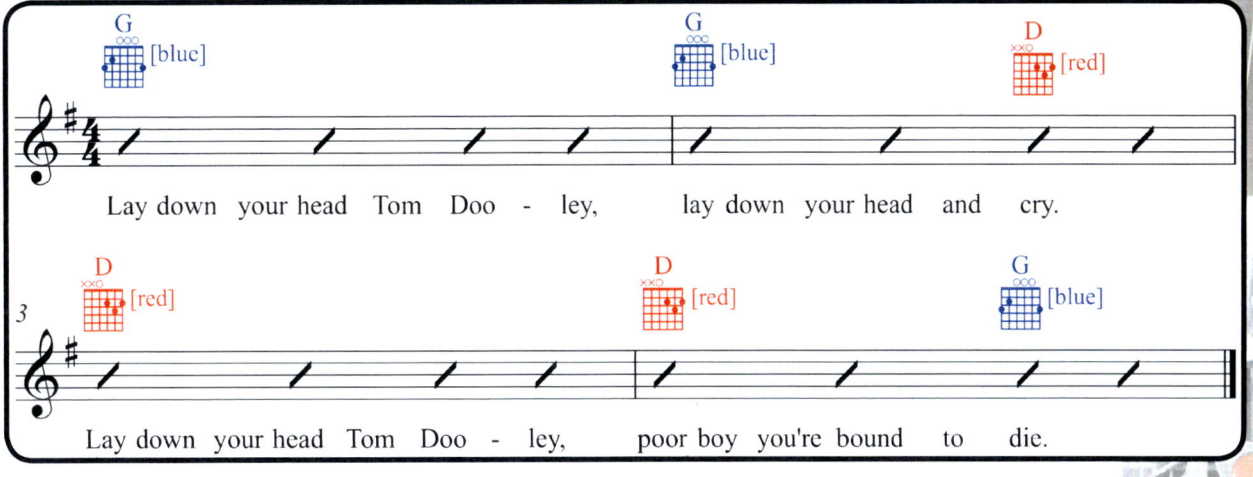

About the Song: "Tom Dooley" is an old Appalachian folk song based on the murder of a woman named Laura Foster by Tom Dula (pronounced Dooley). For his crimes, Tom Dula was convicted and sentenced to death on May 1st, 1868.

Go Tell Aunt Rhodie   2-Chord Song

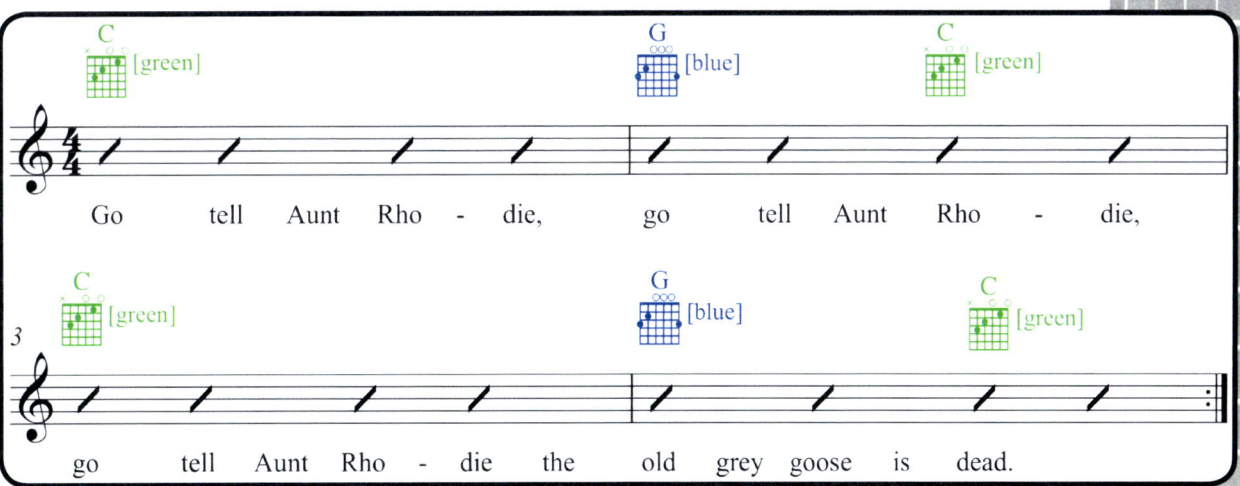

About the Song: "Go Tell Aunt Rhodie" is a folk song with unusual roots. In the 1700's a composer named Rousseau wrote this tune into one of his operas. Eventually people began to put words to it and called it "Go Tell Aunt Rhodie."

Unit 2: Quarter Strum in 3/4 time

Warm-up Note: Use the Quarter Strum pattern to play this warm-up. The chord names are now listed only when you are supposed to change chords, they are not listed in every measure.

Warm-up 2A and 2B

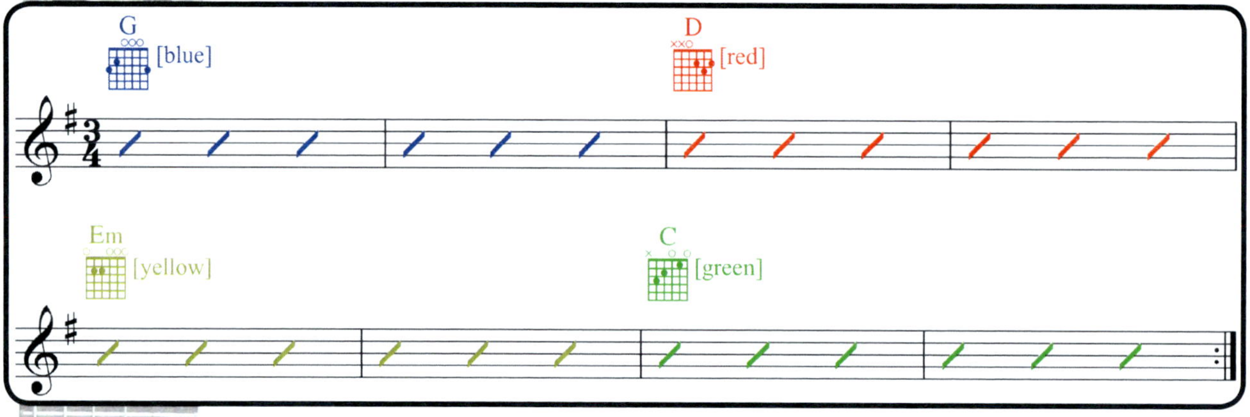

G [blue]　D [red]

Em [yellow]　C [green]

Practice Reminder
Play the correct number of strings for each chord

Play with a clear tone

Additional Warm-up

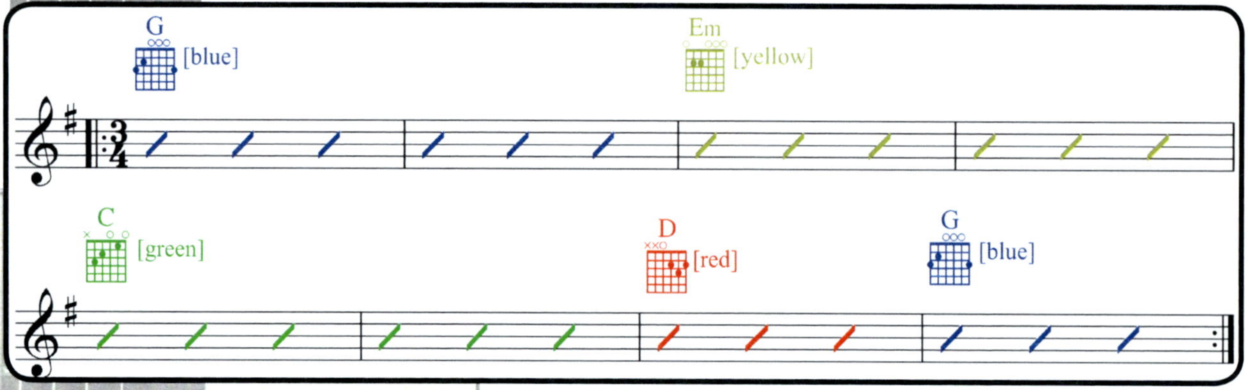

G [blue]　Em [yellow]

C [green]　D [red]　G [blue]

Quarter Strum in 3/4 time

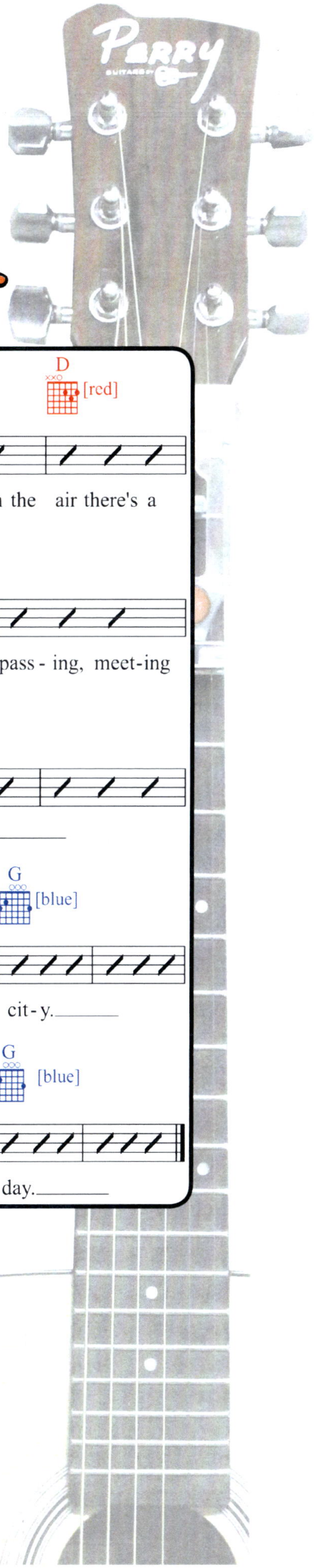

Silver Bells   **3-Chord Song**

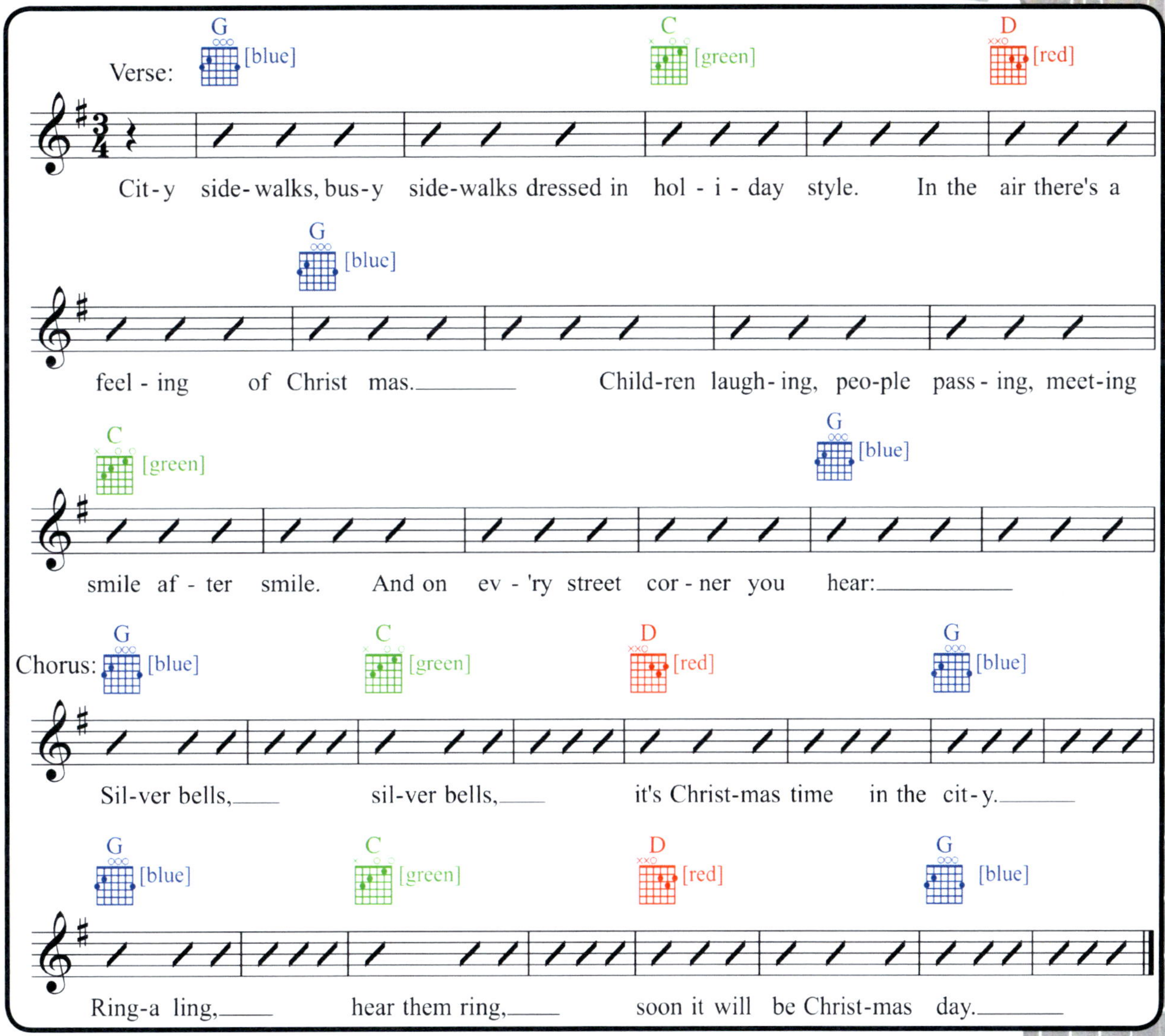

Verse:
G [blue]   C [green]   D [red]

Cit-y side-walks, bus-y side-walks dressed in hol-i-day style. In the air there's a

G [blue]

feel-ing of Christ-mas. Child-ren laugh-ing, peo-ple pass-ing, meet-ing

C [green]   G [blue]

smile af-ter smile. And on ev-'ry street cor-ner you hear:

Chorus: G [blue]   C [green]   D [red]   G [blue]

Sil-ver bells, sil-ver bells, it's Christ-mas time in the cit-y.

G [blue]   C [green]   D [red]   G [blue]

Ring-a ling, hear them ring, soon it will be Christ-mas day.

About the Song: Composed by Jay Livingston and Ray Evans, "Silver Bells" was released in 1951. It was first performed by Bob Hope and Marilyn Maxwell in the motion picture "The Lemon Drop Kid." It was later recorded by Bing Crosby and Carol Richards.

Unit 3: Down/UP Strum

Warm-up Note: Use the Down/Up strum pattern to play this warm-up. Keep your wrist in constant motion to make a good sound. Remember to play the correct number of guitar strings for the different chords.

```
 /  /  /  /  /  /  /  /
 D  U  D  U  D  U  D  U
 1  +  2  +  3  +  4  +
```

Warm-Up 3A

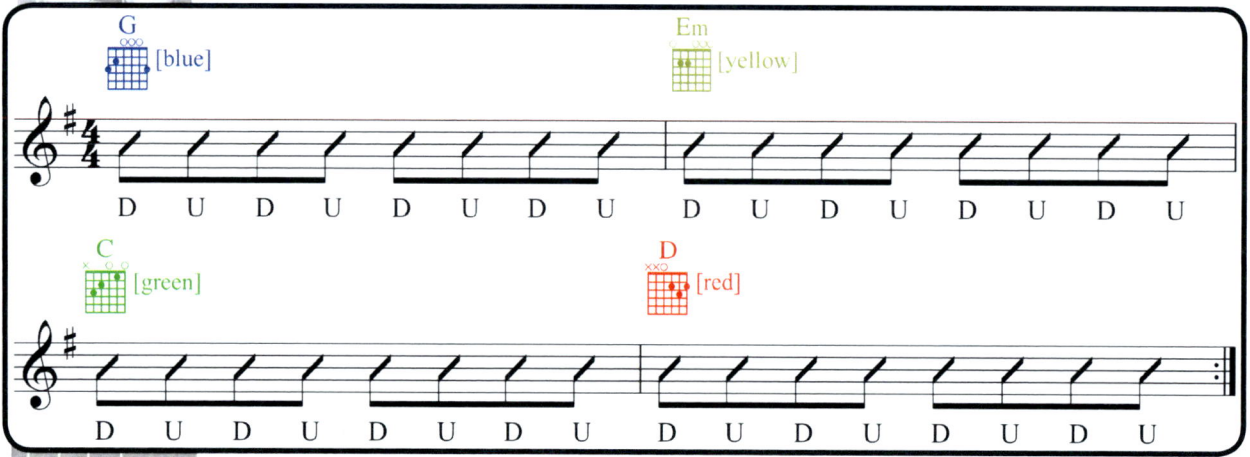

Warm-Up 3B and 3C

Practice Reminder
Keep a steady beat

Pick grip

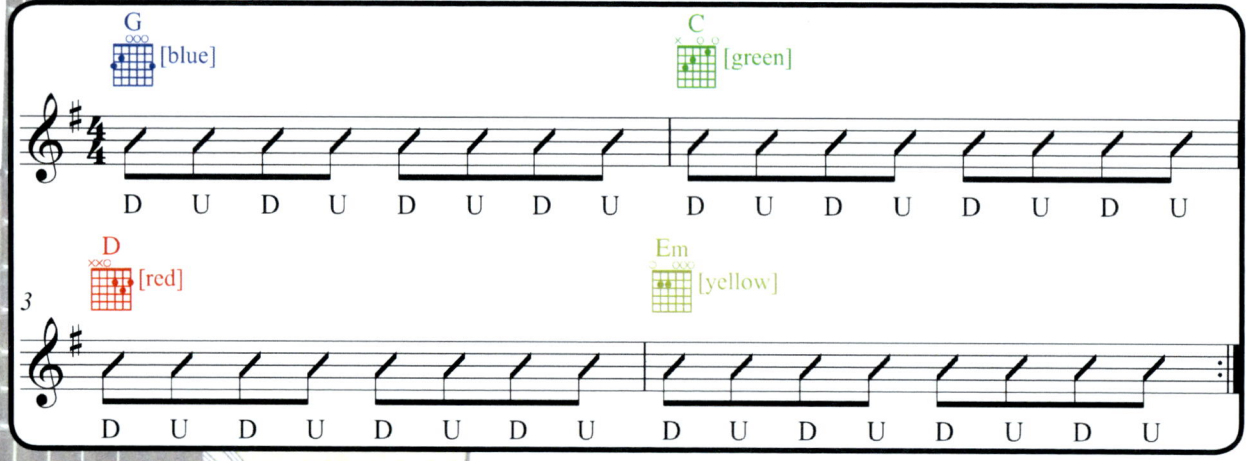

10

Unit 3: Down/UP Strum

Additional Warm-Up

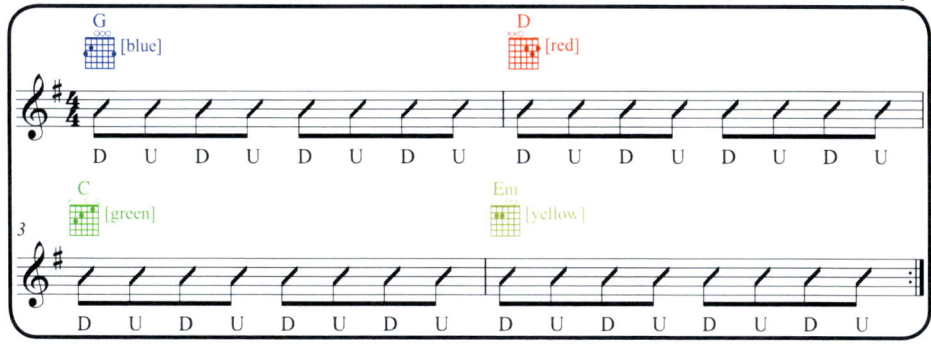

She'll Be Coming Round the Mountain   3- Chord Song

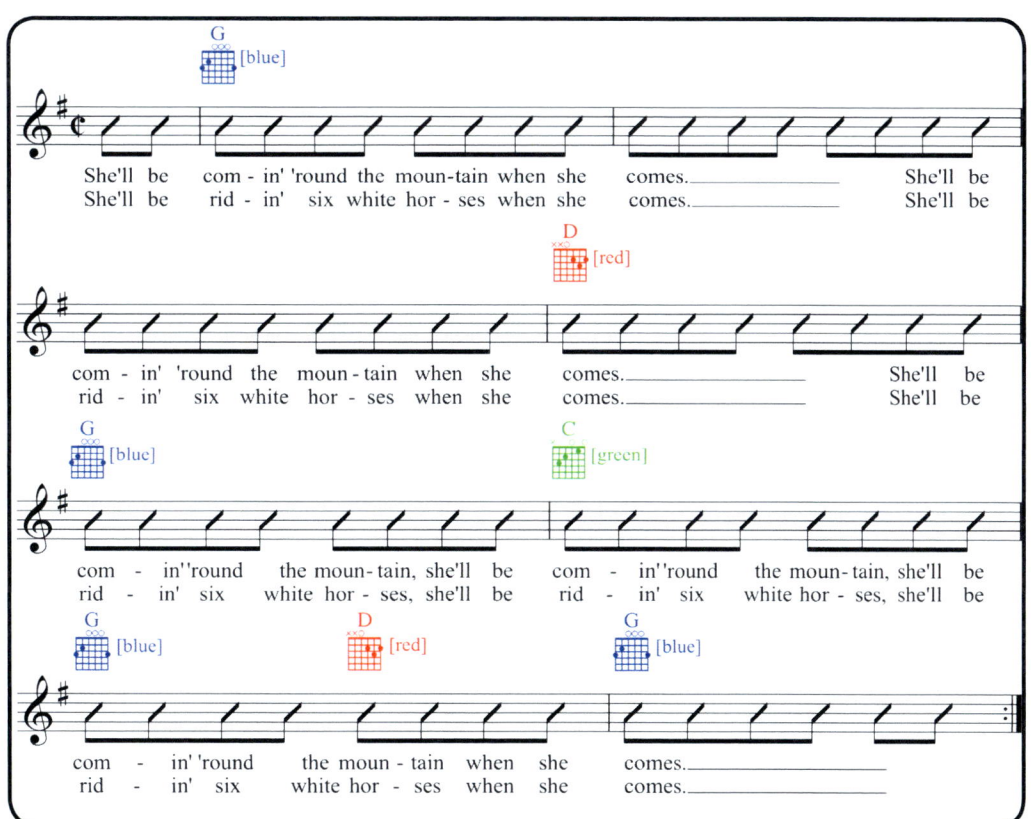

About the Song: "She'll Be coming Round the Mountain" sometimes called 'Coming Round the Mountain' is an American folksong from the 19th century. The first printed edition of this song appears in Carl Sandburg's, The American Songbag (1927). The song was sung by railroad workers in the Midwestern United States in the 1890s.

Unit 4: Pick Strum

Practice Reminder
Pick the correct bass note for each chord

Posture

Warm-up Note: Use the pick strum pattern to play this warm-up. The pick strum adds a bass note before the strum. Here are the bass notes to play with each chord:

G-major and **E-minor** chords
Pick sixth string and strum the bottom five strings
C-major Chord
Pick fifth string and strum the bottom four strings
D-major Chord
Pick fourth string and strum the bottom three strings

Warm-Up 4A

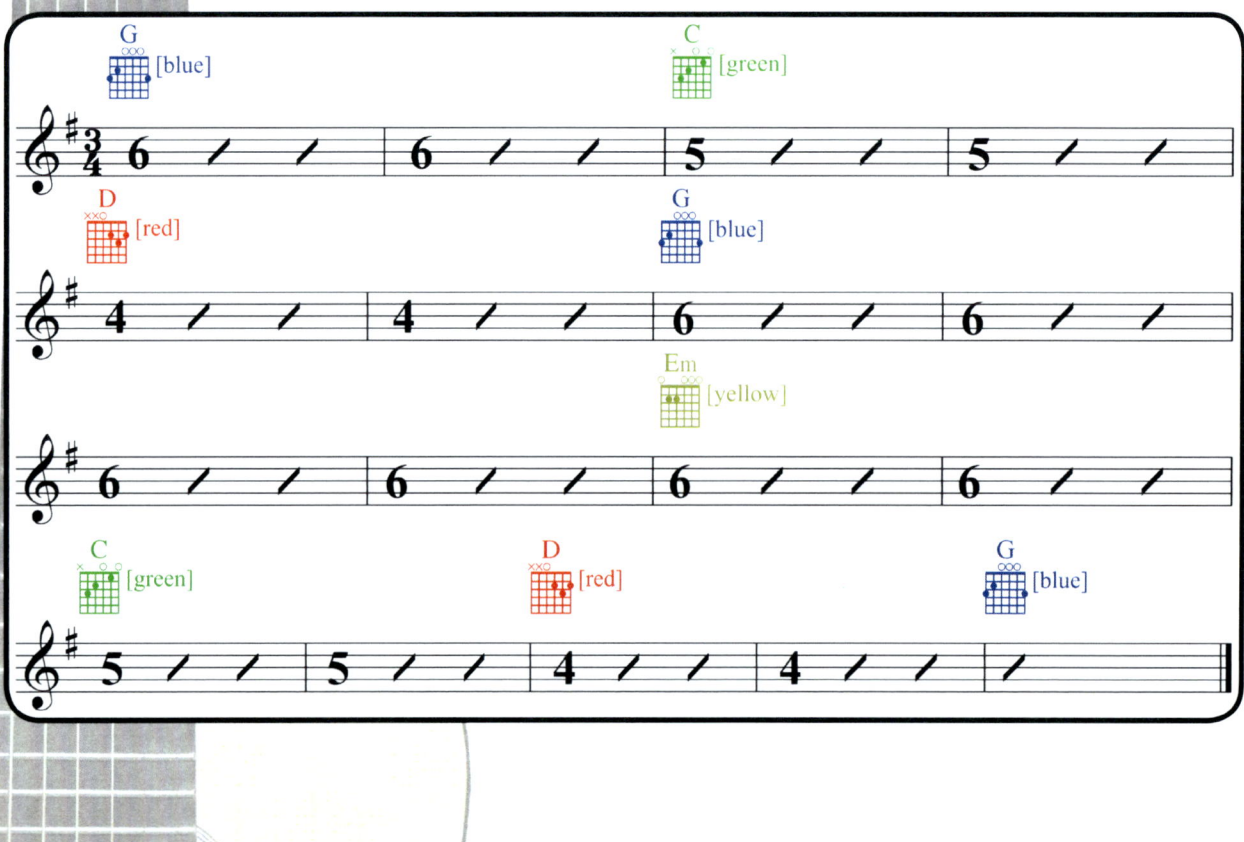

Pick Strum

About the Song: "On Top of Old Smokey" is a traditional folk song that rose to the top of the record charts with The Weavers 1951 recording. While there have been many parodies written for this song, the most popular is On Top of Spaghetti.

Unit 5: Alternate Pick Strum

Warm-up Note: Use the alternate pick strum to play this warm-up. Add the root note and the fifth note of the chord to the strum pattern. Here are the strings to play with each chord:

G-major = 6 and 4
E-minor = 6 and 5
C-major = 5 and 4
D-major = 4 and 5

Warm-Up 5A and 5B

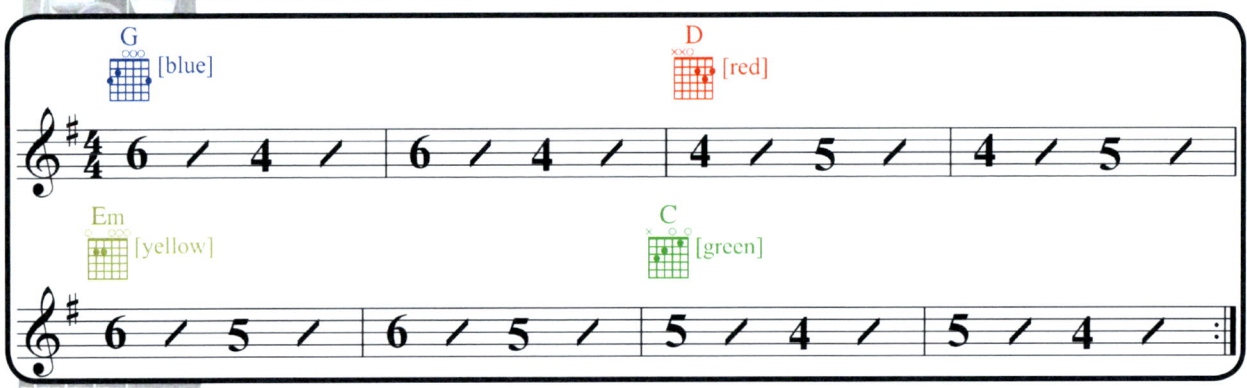

Additional Warm-Up

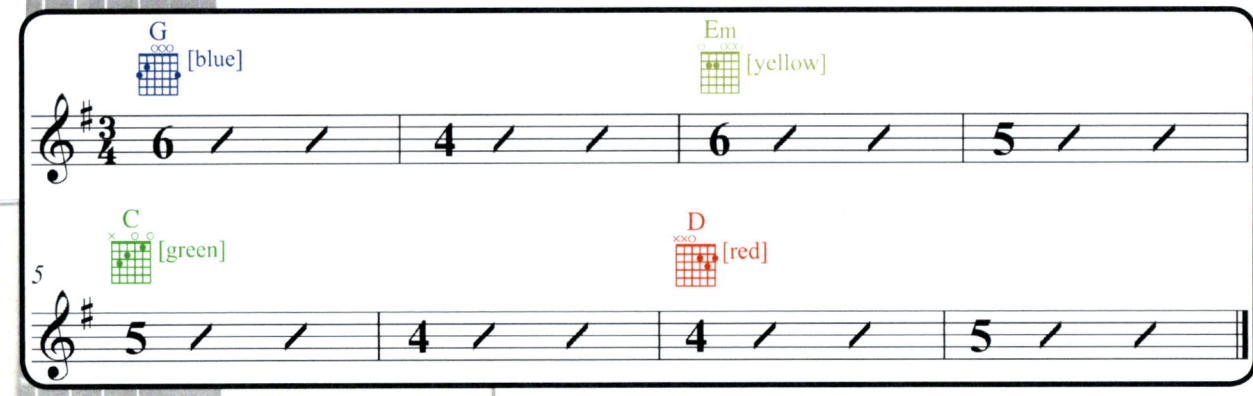

14

Alternate Pick Strum

Practice Reminder
Pick the correct root note and fifth note of the chord

Bad Moon Rising   3-Chord Song

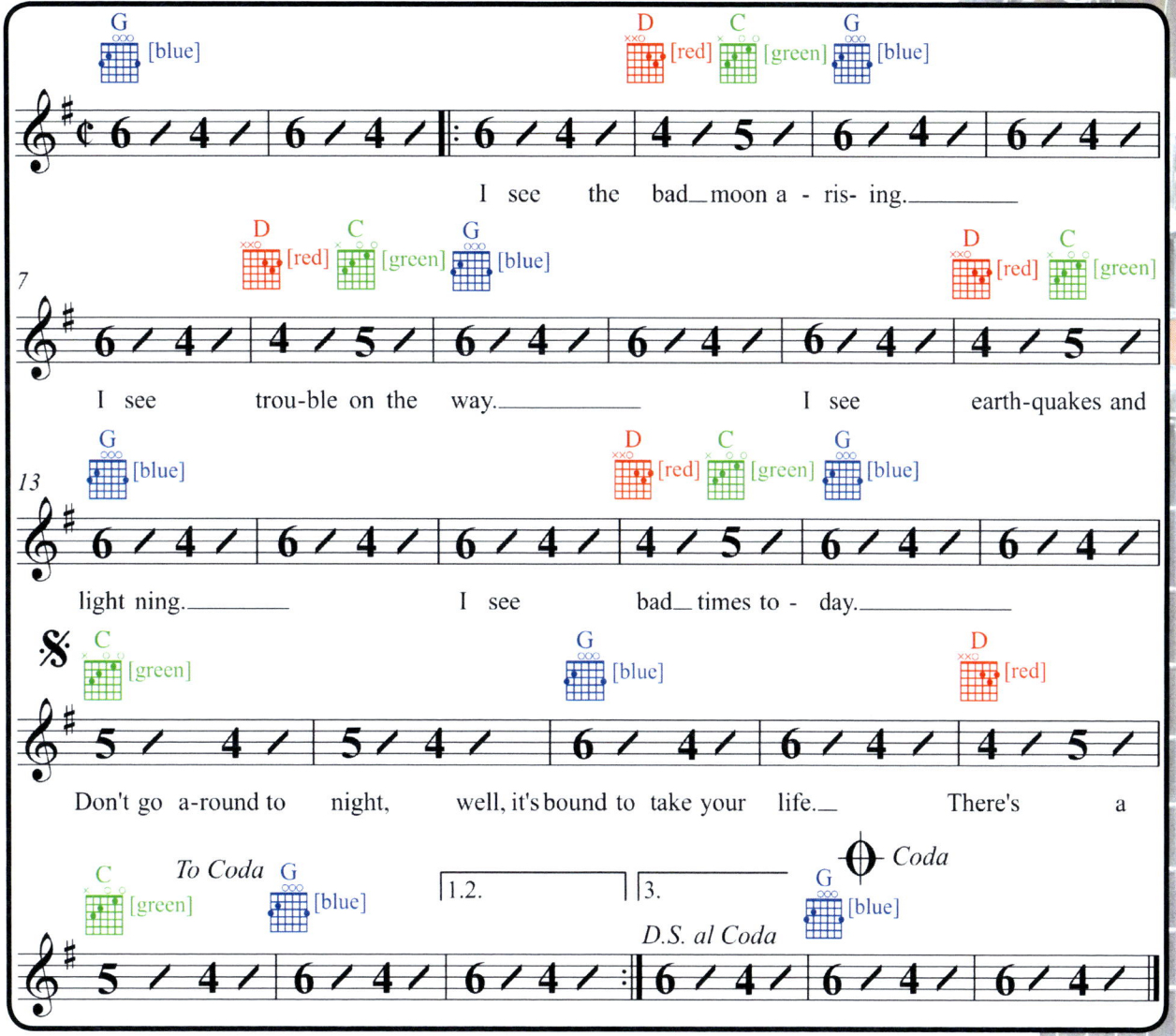

About the Song: "Bad Moon Rising" was released in 1969 by Creedence Clearwater Revival. The track was written by John Fogerty and was the lead single from their album Green River. The track reached #2 on the Billboard hot 100 singles chart and #1 on the UK singles chart for three weeks in September 1969.

15

Unit 6: Pop Strum

Warm-up Note: Use the pop strum pattern to play this warm-up. Below is a written description of the pattern:
D = downstrum   **U** = upstrum
(D) = downward motion with no strum
(U) = upward motion with no strum

```
  /    /   /    /   /    /
D (U)  D   U  (D)  U    D   U
1 (+)  2   +  (3)  +    4   +
```

Warm-Up 6A and 6B

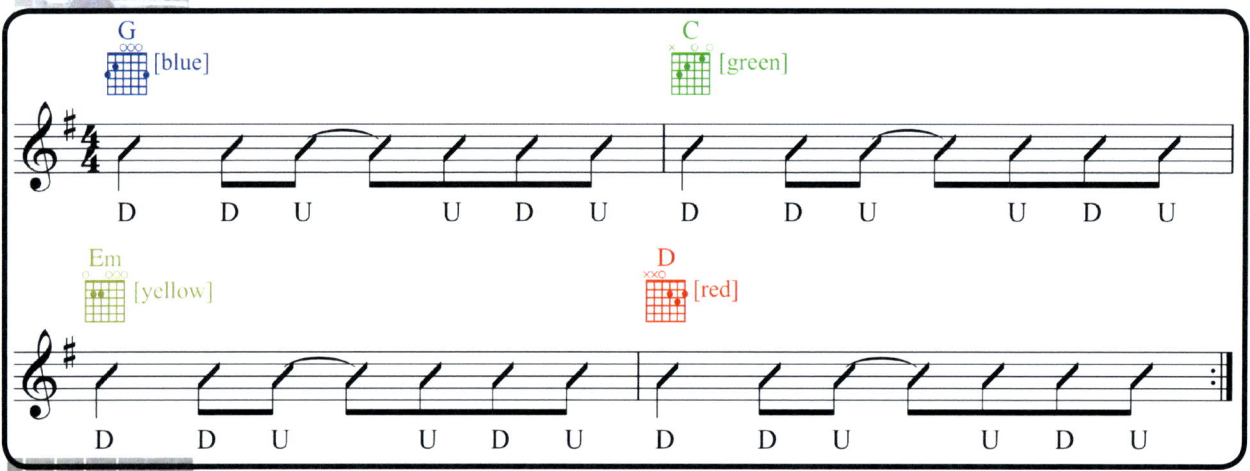

Additional Warm-Up

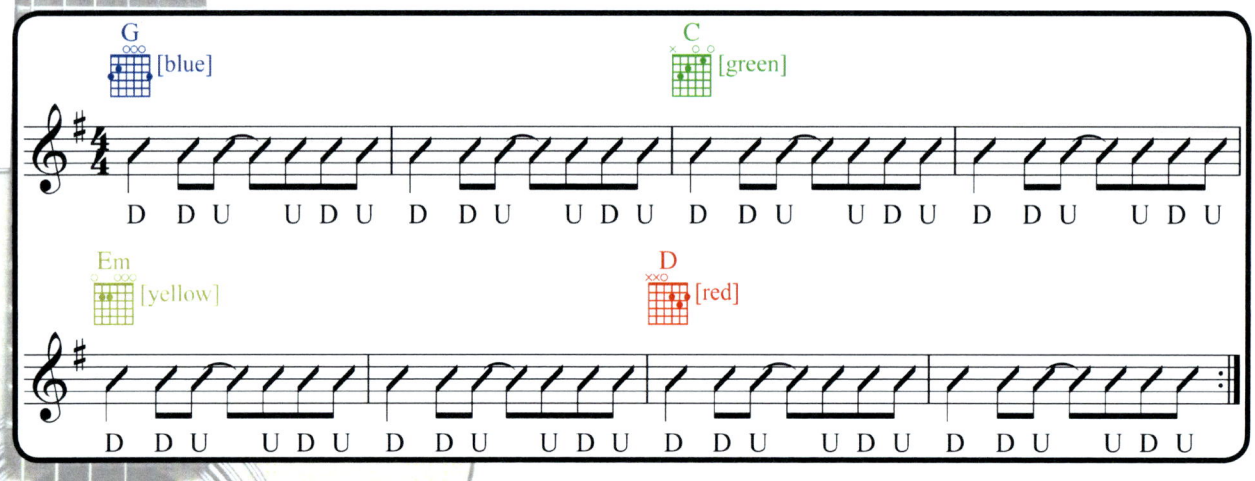

Pop Strum

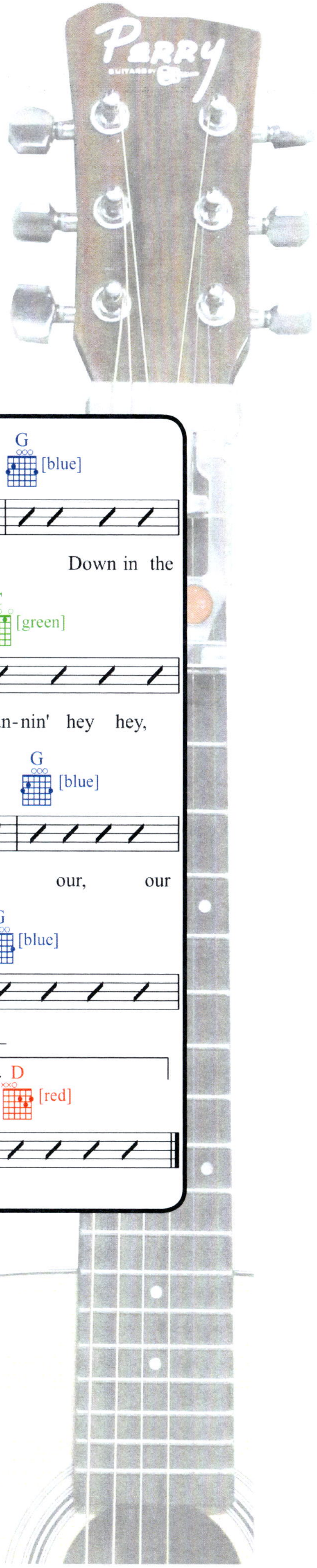

Practice Reminder
Produce a bright and clear tone on the guitar

Pick grip

Brown Eyed Girl   2-Chord Song

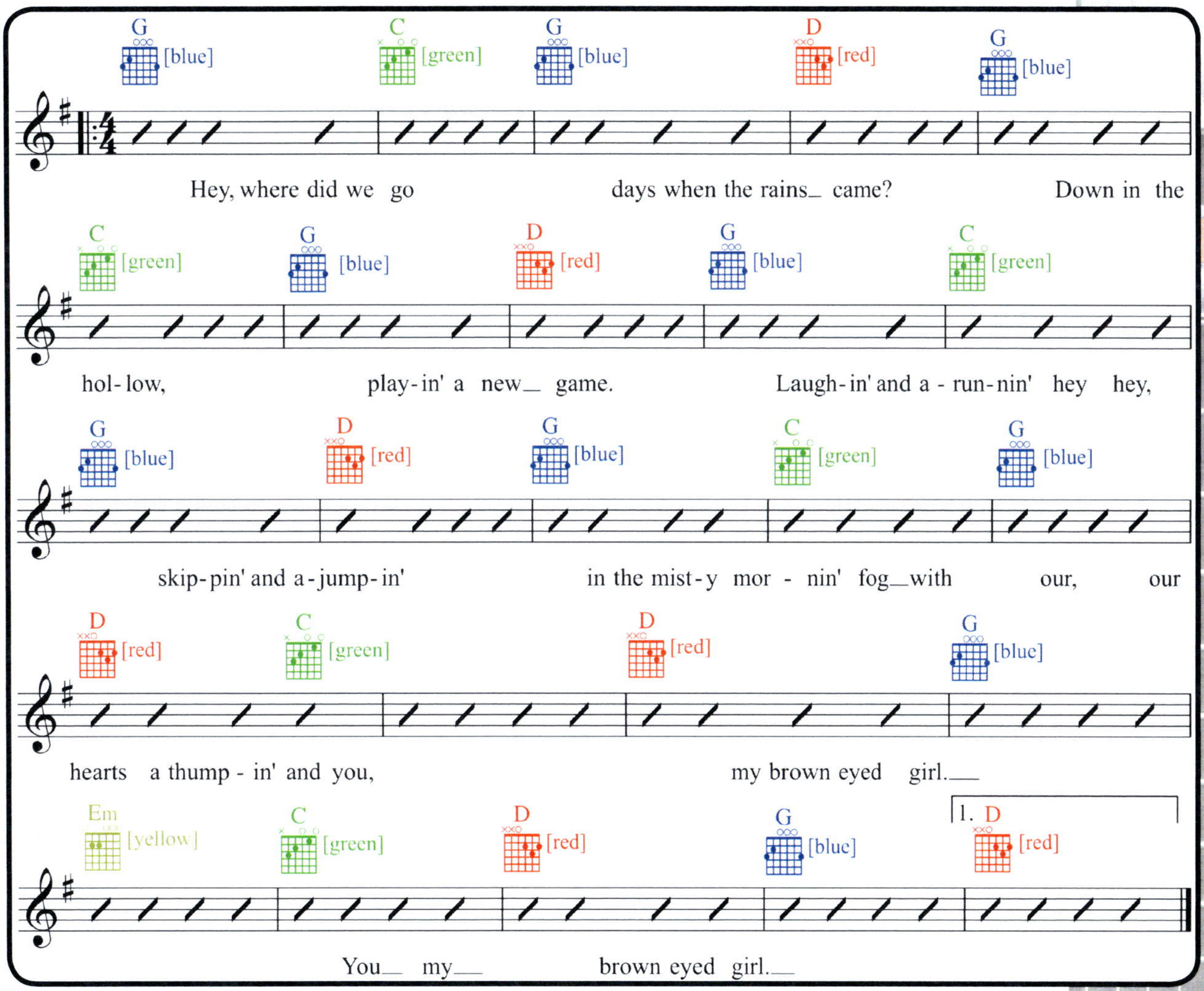

| G [blue] | C [green] | G [blue] | D [red] | G [blue] |

Hey, where did we go   days when the rains came?   Down in the

| C [green] | G [blue] | D [red] | G [blue] | C [green] |

hol-low,   play-in' a new game.   Laugh-in' and a-run-nin' hey hey,

| G [blue] | D [red] | G [blue] | C [green] | G [blue] |

skip-pin' and a-jump-in'   in the mist-y mor-nin' fog with   our, our

| D [red] | C [green] | D [red] | G [blue] |

hearts a thump-in' and you,   my brown eyed girl.

| Em [yellow] | C [green] | D [red] | G [blue] | 1. D [red] |

You my   brown eyed girl.

About the Song: Recorded in 1967, Van Morrison's classic Brown Eyed Girl is as popular today as when it was first released. A song about growing up and reflection, Brown Eyed Girl is often included in conversations about songs that helped shape rock and roll.

Unit 7: Progress Check

Practice Reminder
Play the correct number of strings when you strum each chord

Warm-up Note: You are now able to play the Quarter Strum, Down/Up Strum, Pick Strum, and Alternate Pick Strum patterns. Use these warm-ups to review each pattern and prepare for your playing test.

Warm-Up 7A- Quarter, Down/Up, Pop Strum Review

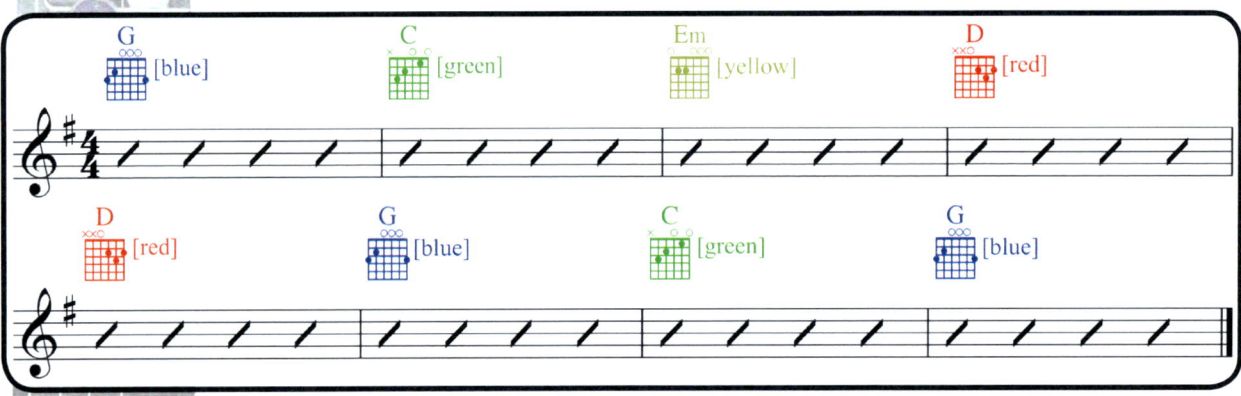

Warm-Up 7B- Pick Strum Review

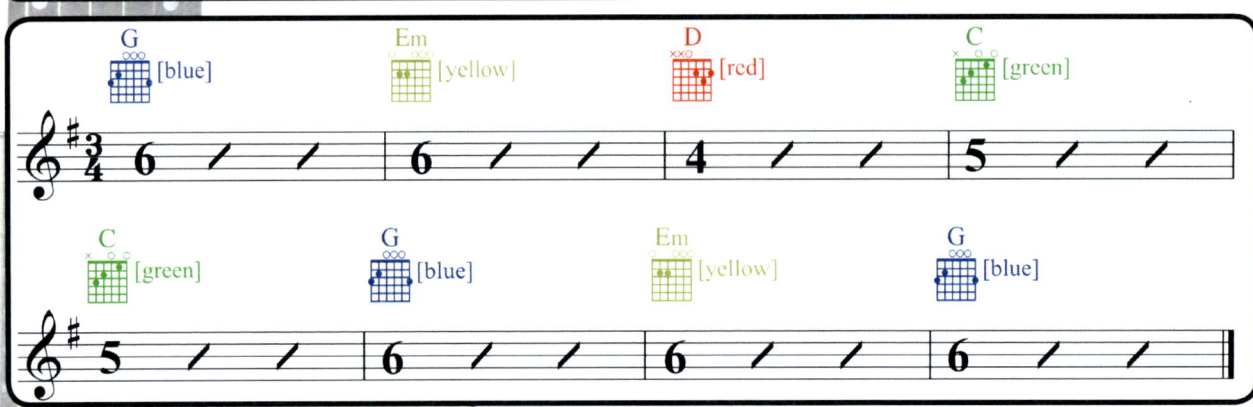

Unit 7: Progress Check

Warm-Up 7C- Alternate Pick Strum

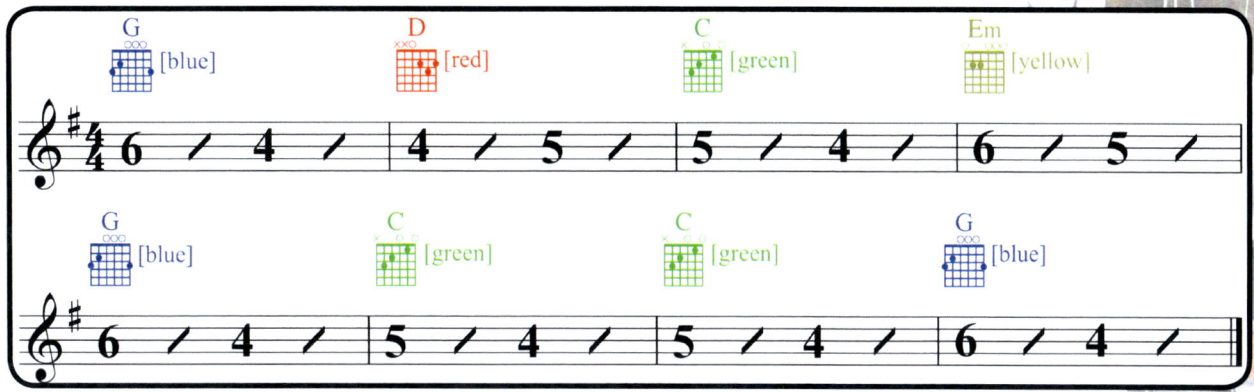

What does practicing look like?

- Play the song over and over again until you know it really well and can easily make the chord changes.

- Play the song over and over again until you know it really well and can easily make the chord changes.

- When you make a mistake, go back and play that part again until you can do it correctly.

- First practice your song at a slow tempo (60-70bpm) and then go faster when you know it well.

How do I know if I am playing correctly?

- Use your 12-point Playing Checklist as a guide to know if you are consistently playing the guitar correctly.

- Ask a friend to watch you play and give pointers of how you can improve.

Final Activity: Watch the last chapter of the DVD and the fairwell from Travis Perry.

Notes